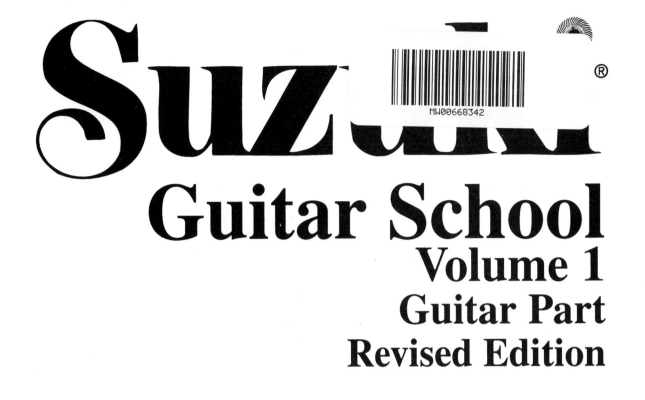

Suzuki
Guitar School
Volume 1
Guitar Part
Revised Edition

© 1991, 1999 Dr. SHINICHI SUZUKI
Sole Publisher for the World excluding Japan: SUMMY-BIRCHARD INC.
Exclusive Print Rights Administered by ALFRED PUBLISHING CO., INC.
All Rights Reserved

ISBN 0-87487-388-6

INTRODUCTION

Summy-Birchard Inc. is proud to be able to present this material for you.

The development of this work is the result of an ongoing study and has been compiled, tested and revised many times over the course of several years. This, however, will continue to be an ongoing process. Interested individuals should get in touch with the publisher at the indicated address.

FOR THE STUDENT: This material is part of the worldwide Suzuki Method of teaching. Companion recordings should be used with these publications. In addition, there are guitar accompaniment books that go along with this material.

FOR THE TEACHER: In order to be an effective Suzuki teacher, a great deal of ongoing education is required. Your national Suzuki association provides this for its membership. Teachers are encouraged to become members of their national Suzuki associations and maintain a teacher training schedule, in order to remain current, via institutes, short and long term programs. You are also encouraged to join the International Suzuki Association.

FOR THE PARENT: Credentials are essential for any teacher that you choose. We recommend you ask your teacher for his or her credentials, especially listing those relating to training in the Suzuki Method. The Suzuki Method experience should be a positive one, where there exists a wonderful, fostering relationship between child, parent and teacher. So choosing the right teacher is of the utmost importance.

In order to obtain more information about the Suzuki Method, please contact your country's Suzuki Association, the International Suzuki Association at 3-10-15 Fukashi, Matsumoto City 390, Japan, the Suzuki Association of the Americas, 1900 Folsom, #101, Boulder, Colorado 80302, or Summy-Birchard Inc., c/o Warner Bros. Publications Inc., 15800 N.W. 48th Avenue, Miami, Florida 33014, for current Associations' addresses.

CONTENTS

Suzuki Guitar Method

Principles of Study and Guidance

Four Essential Points for Teachers and Parents
1. The child should listen to reference recordings every day at home to develop musical sensitivity. Rapid progress depends on this listening.

2. Tonalization, or the production of beautiful tone, should be stressed in the lesson and at home.

3. Constant attention should be given to correct posture and proper hand positioning.

4. Parents and teachers should strive to motivate the child so he will enjoy practicing correctly at home.

Through his experience in teaching young children for over thirty years, Dr. Suzuki has become thoroughly convinced that musical ability can be fully cultivated in every child if the above four points are faithfully observed.

Musical ability is not an inborn talent but an ability that can be developed. Any child who is properly trained can develop musical ability, just as all children develop the ability to speak their mother tongue. To insure the happy, effective progress of students, the four essential points listed above should be carefully observed and put to continual use in the home and studio.

Just as the alphabet is not taught when children first learn their mother language, so music reading should not be included in the study of the guitar until children have sufficiently developed their musical sensitivity, playing skill, and memory. Even after acquiring the ability to read music, however, the children should, as a rule, play from memory during lessons.

Education for Musical Sensitivity

Every day, children should listen to the recordings of the music they are currently studying. This listening helps them make rapid progress. It is the most important factor in the development of musical ability. Those children who have not had enough listening will lack musical sensitivity.

Tonalization for Beautiful Tone

Just as vocalization is studied in vocal music, tonalization on the guitar is introduced as an essential element of study. Tonalization should always be included at each lesson and should be a part of the daily practice at home.

Group Lessons

The group lesson is an extremely effective instructional and motivational tool. The students progress remarkably while enjoying these lessons. Dr. Suzuki recommends that group lessons be held once a week or at least twice a month.

Private Lessons to Develop Ability

A child should not proceed to a new piece simply because he has learned the fingering or notes of the present one. His ability must be cultivated further as he plays his piece. It should be said to the child, "Now that you know the notes, we can start the very important work of developing your ability, " and then procedures may be made to improve his tone, movements, and musical ability.

The repertoire found in these volumes has been carefully chosen to provide an enjoyable path towards technical proficiency. It is important that when a child can perform piece A satisfactorily and is given a new piece, B, he should not drop A but should practice both A and B at the same time. By continuously reviewing and refining pieces that he knows, as new pieces are added, he will develop his ability to a higher degree.

Parents and children should always observe the private lessons of other children. Lessons should vary in length according to the needs of the child. Sometimes a child may have a short lesson, stop and watch another child, and then return for more instruction.

Basic Technique

The establishment of an attentive but relaxed body position is extremely important. A comfortable but firm chair should be used. The student's particular body dimensions will determine the proper height of the footstool and chair. The student should sit on the front edge of the chair with the left foot elevated and the right foot placed securely on the floor. The left, lower leg should remain vertical.

The shoulders should remain down and relaxed with the torso straight and balanced but not rigid. The waist of the guitar rests on the left leg with the right arm draped gently at the lower bout.

Fig. 1. The guitar contacts the body at four points:

1. The left leg.
2. The center of the chest.
3. The inner right upper leg.
4. The right forearm near the elbow.

The Right Arm and Hand

Attention should be paid to the positioning and movements of the upper arm, shoulder, elbow and forearm before emphasis is given to the hands and fingers. The hand should remain a natural extension of the right arm. It should have a roundness (fingers curved) with the thumb slightly forward of the fingers.

Fig. 2. Correct Right Arm Position with the forearm resting on the lower bout.

Fig. 3. Preparation for the G string rest stroke.

Exercises for Changing Strings

Place arm and hand as in Fig. 2. Change strings quickly.
All finger combinations (im, mi, ia, ai, ma, am) should eventually be used.

The Left Arm and Hand

A symmetrical, balanced left hand position should be established. The palm of the left hand should be parallel to the lower edge of the fingerboard. The wrist should remain straight or gently arched. The arm and hand should be relaxed with little pressure from the thumb when depressing strings with the fingertips.

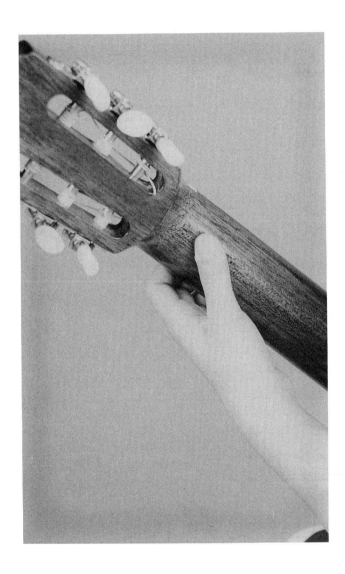

Fig. 4. The left hand thumb should be flat and favoring the left side of the hand. The wrist should remain essentially straight.

Fig. 5. The correct left hand position is balanced, with the palm essentially parallel to the neck of the instrument. The third finger is on the B string.

1
Twinkle, Twinkle, Little Star Variations

S. Suzuki

Variation A

Variation B

Variation C

Variation D

Variation E

Theme

Tonalization in G #1

Be sure to alternate the right hand fingers.

2
Lightly Row

Folk Song

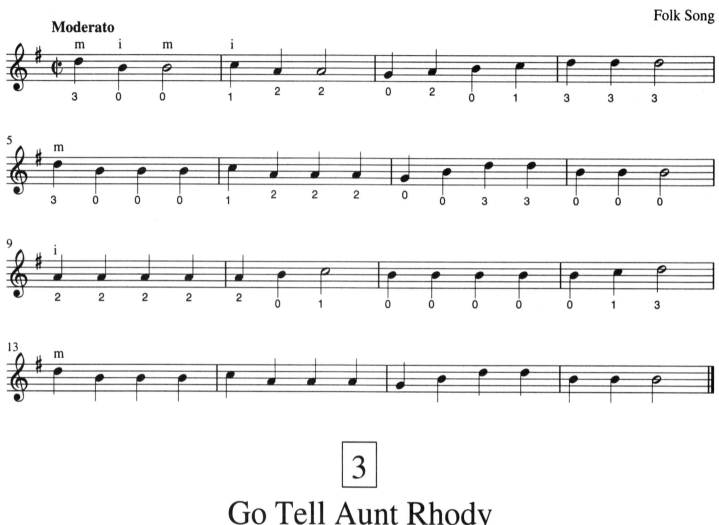

3
Go Tell Aunt Rhody

Folk Song

4
Song of the Wind

Moderato

Folk Song

5

May Song

Allegro moderato

Folk Song

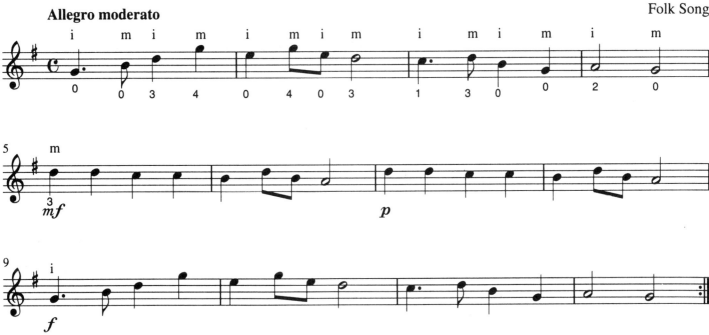

Tonalization in G #2

No. 1

No. 2

6

Allegretto

M. Giuliani

Preliminary Exercise

Pos. II

7
Perpetual Motion

S. Suzuki

Variation

8

Rigadoon

H. Purcell

9

Are You Sleeping, Brother John?

Folk Song/Round

Preliminary Thumb Stroke Exercise

Rest the fingers on the G string.
The Thumb touches the Index Finger after each stroke.

Tonalizations in D Major

No. 1

No. 2

No. 3

Review these considerations regularly:

- The responsibility of motivating the child belongs to the parent and the teacher.

- Listening to the recordings is essential to rapid progress and the development of musical sensitivity.

- Correct posture, and proper arm, hand and finger placement should receive constant attention.

- Tonalization, or the production of beautiful tone, should always be stressed.

Preliminary Exercises for the Fingers and the Thumb

1. Be sure to keep the right hand steady.
2. Use alternate fingers with the thumb, (i p i p, m p m p, i p m p, m p i p, etc. . . . .)

10

French Folk Song

Folk Song

11
Tanz

J. Führman

12
Tanz

J.C. Bach

13

With Steady Hands

F. Longay

Tonalizations in A Major

No. 1

No. 2

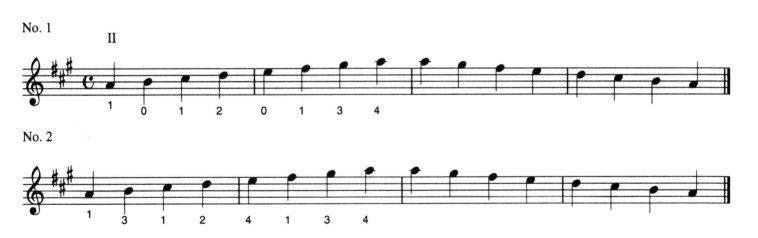

Remember:

• Each piece should be thoroughly mastered before moving to the next.

• Review learned pieces on a regular basis.

14

Meadow Minuet

F. Longay